This book belongs to:

_____

Age: _____

My First
Dictionary

♯ · ♯ · ♯

CORRUPTING YOUNG MINDS

ONE WORD AT A TIME

♯ · ♯ · ♯

DEY ST.
AN IMPRINT OF
WILLIAM MORROW *PUBLISHERS*

My First
Dictionary

¤ · ¤ · ¤

ROSS HORSLEY

DEY ST.

MY FIRST DICTIONARY. Copyright © 2011 by Ross Horsley. All rights reserved. Printed in China.

FIRST EDITION

Designed by Betty Lew

Library of Congress Cataloging-in-Publication data is available upon request.

ISBN 978-0-06-200001-9

18 19 20 SCP 10 9 8 7 6 5 4 3 2

My First
Dictionary

in•tro•duc•tion *noun*
(BEGINNING) ˈin.trəˈdəkshən

What does it mean if Daddy says he's going to **abandon** you? How long do you have left if the doctors have given you **zero** chance of survival? You'll find all the answers right here in *My First Dictionary*, the educational tool that opens up your ears to a whole new world of "grown-up speak."

If you've already mastered the basics of reading and writing, no doubt you're sick of hearing about Peter playing with his **balls** and Susie stroking her **puppies**. Now it's time to learn some words that will *really* help you to understand what Mommy and Daddy are whispering about behind that closed bedroom door.

Find out why you should act **quickly** if you want to be included in a dying relative's will . . . How special pills can make you feel **mellow** . . . And what it means if a hit man tells you you're his latest **assignment**.

Make *My First Dictionary* **your** first point of reference for these and many other useful words.

A

ABANDON

Father is trying to **abandon** us.

He is trying to start a new life without us.

ABOVE

The eagle is **above** Chico.

It is over, Chico.

ADAPTABLE

Harry's hook is not as **adaptable** as his hand was before the accident.

It cannot perform as many functions, especially when it comes to pleasuring himself.

ADULT

An **adult** is a grown-up person.

When I am an **adult**, I want to be just like Uncle Max.

Except I won't let the police catch me.

ADVANCE

Linda's foster parents apologized in **advance**.

They apologized before subjecting her to eleven years of abuse and neglect.

AFRAID

Sammy is **afraid**.

He is scared.

Everything looks funny since he ate the mushrooms.

ALIKE

Tommy and Granny's drinks are **alike**.

They look similar.

If only Tommy could remember which one he put the arsenic in.

ALMOST

Martin is **almost** ready for another vodka.

He is nearly ready now.

ALONE

Lois is **alone** in the house.

She is the only person in the house.

. . . Isn't she?

ALSO

A drum makes a sound when you hit it with a stick.

A baby **also** makes a sound when you hit it with a stick.

ALWAYS

Spot **always** finds his way home.

He comes back every time we dump him.

ANTICIPATION

Tommy is filled with **anticipation**.

He is filled with expectation.

Any minute now the piranhas he released will reach Jenny.

APOLOGIZE

Harry will **apologize** to Wilma.

He will say that he is sorry for giving her syphilis.

ASSIGNMENT

The hit man has a new **assignment**.

He has a new task to carry out.

ATTENTION

Ray will do anything to get Father's **attention**.

He will do anything to get Father to notice him.

Father's **attention** is worth the splintered fibula and permanent limp.

BACKFIRED

Lucille's plan **backfired**.

It had the opposite effect of what she intended.

Her teacher actually gave her a *lower* grade after receiving oral sex from her during detention.

BACKWARD

Trudy's dress is on **backward.**

Her dress is on back-to-front.

Why does this always seem to happen when she wakes up at Uncle Rory's?

BE

Joyce wants to **be** Mary.

She wants to look like Mary, dress like Mary, and act like Mary.

And she will kill anyone who gets in the way.

BECAUSE

Nancy drinks **because** it is the only time she feels like anyone cares about her.

That is the reason why she drinks.

BETTER, BEST

Baby got a good present for Christmas.

Angus got a **better** present because he is older.

Marsha got the **best** present because she has cancer.

BIDE

Gloria will **bide** her time.

She will wait for the right moment to make them pay.

BITTERSWEET

Hilary's sled ride is **bittersweet**.

It is both happy and sad.

Inducing miscarriage ought not to be so exhilarating.

BLESSING

Every day seems like a **blessing**.

Every day seems like a gift when you have an inoperable brain tumor.

BLISTER

Jack has a **blister**.

It is a sore caused by too much rubbing.

BORED

We are **bored** with the museum.

We are tired of coming here.

We wish Mother would find somewhere else to pick up men.

BRAVERY

Barbara dared Michael to prove his **bravery**.

She dared Michael to prove his courage by running across the freeway while blindfolded.

BRUSH, BRUSHING

Judy is using a **brush**.

She is **brushing** her hair.

She must **brush** it exactly 100 times or something bad will happen.

BURDEN, BURDENS

A **burden** is a source of worry or stress.

Old people are usually **burdens**.

C

CALM

We will **calm** Spot down.

We will soothe him.

He must be nice and still before we make the first incision.

CARE

Mother makes Father's tea with **care**.

She makes a special effort to get it right.

Otherwise, it will end up being thrown in her face again.

CELEBRATE

The people **celebrate** in the street.

They make merry in the street.

That is the end of Old Mister Crenshaw.

CHANCE

There is a **chance** that we may see Father.

There is a possibility that he may escape if the rumors of a prison riot are true.

CHAOS

cannabis

bondage enthusiast

Louisa's party has descended into **chaos**.

It has become disordered.

There is vomit in the fish tank, an orgy going on in the bedroom, and no sign of Baby.

If only Louisa had not advertised it on Facebook.

vodka

stripper

slut

CHRISTEN

Jim will **christen** the valley in honor of his pony.

He will name it Pumpin' Pony-Sex Valley.

CLEAR

Edward's proposal was **clear**.

He explained exactly which part of Andrea's anatomy he intended to remove, and left no ambiguity about where he would be defecating.

CLONE

A **clone** is a copy of a person.

Would you know if your daddy had been replaced by a **clone**?

CLOSE, CLOSER

"Come and sit **close** to me," Mr. May says to Cindy.

"That's it, right next to me . . . **Closer** . . ."

COAX

Jane will **coax** Father into telling her another bedtime story.

She will do everything she can to persuade him.

COINCIDENCE

William is sure it is a **coincidence**.

He is sure it is simple chance that his mother happened to sleep over at the principal's house the night before he was accepted into this school.

COLOR, COLORS

The **color** of an item is one quality of its appearance.

Red, orange, yellow, green, and blue are all **colors**.

red

orange

yellow

green

blue

EXERCISE

Can you match the following with their colors?

1. Vomit following pork dinner with gin.

2. Cold dead lips of a corpse.

3. Aftermath of shark attack.

4. Running out of Valium.

5. Fit of rage caused by repressed memories of incest.

COMBINE

Rodrigo's magic act allows him to **combine** his talents.

It allows him to mix his talents for magic tricks and predatory pedophilia.

CONCEAL

The books **conceal** a secret door.

They hide the door to Daddy's S&M dungeon.

CONCISE

Oliver's writing is **concise**.

His death threats are short, yet notably graphic in their detail.

CONSULT

Jack wishes that Mother would **consult** him.

He wishes she would ask him before borrowing his porn.

CONVENIENT

Something is **convenient** if it saves time and effort.

Mother finds the new washing machine **convenient**.

She can give Baby a bath in half the time.

CORN

Corn is an edible grain.

Judy loves **corn** on the cob.

Someday she may even find
out what it tastes like.

COUCH

A **couch** is a piece of furniture.

Father has taken to
sleeping on
the **couch** ever
since Mother
gave him a
black eye.

COUPON

Hilary has a **coupon**.

It is a piece of paper that ensures a discount.

Hilary can use the **coupon** to save 10% on a back-alley abortion.

COVER

Dad uses a picture to **cover** the peephole.

The peephole is hidden behind a picture on the other side of the bathroom wall.

CREATIVE

Verna is **creative**.

She finds new ways to do and look at things.

Where some see a jump rope, she sees a garrote.

CRISIS

A **crisis** is an emotional upheaval.

Chico is having an identity crisis.

CROP

We are picking apples.

We have a fine apple **crop**.

When we have collected twenty more baskets, we will be allowed a break.

CURIOUS

Virginia is a **curious** child.

She is interested in a great many things.

CUT, CUTS

Caroline has **cut** her finger.

She usually **cuts** her inner thigh.

DECIDE

Carrie is not sure which of the boys is the father.

Sleeping with each of them one more time will help her to **decide**.

DELUSION

Grandma is suffering from a **delusion**.

She has a false belief.

She thinks she is no longer inside the nursing facility.

DESCRIPTION

Alma gave a **description** of the man who touched her in the park.

He had a yellow hat, big feet, and a red nose.

DISILLUSIONED

Peggy is **disillusioned**.

She has seen the sad truth.

Mr. May is cheating on her with most of the other girls in class.

DISOWN

Mother has decided to **disown** Patty.

She wants nothing to do with Patty or the black baby.

DISPOSE

Bessie will **dispose** of the rat poison.

She will get rid of the rat poison after preparing Pat's last breakfast.

DISRUPTION

Daniel caused a **disruption**.

He caused a disturbance at the funeral.

DISTRAUGHT

Mother is **distraught**.

She is very upset.

Not only are the twins missing, but so is the expensive stroller.

DONE

Mother is **done** cleaning out the fishbowl.

She is through with it.

DOT, DOTS

A **dot** is a small circle.

There are red **dots** on Lena's dress.

She should have stepped away when she pulled the trigger.

DOUBTFUL

If something is **doubtful**, it is very unlikely.

It is **doubtful** that Jeff will get Jenny pregnant by doing that.

DRAG

Marsha has become a **drag**.

She has lost all sense of fun since she started the chemotherapy.

DRAW, DRAWING
DREW, DRAWN

Allison can **draw**.

She is **drawing** a picture

She **drew** one yesterday.

She has **drawn** two pictures.

The psychiatrists keep them in a file.

DURING

During means throughout the existence of something.

Carolyn retreats into her own world **during** Mommy and Daddy's violent arguments.

DWINDLED

Our choir is less.

Our number has **dwindled**.

Ever since Jennifer's herpes rekindled.

E

EARLY

School finished **early** today.

It finished before the usual time.

EFFORT

Finding the blackness takes **effort**.

It takes hard work.

Jean is on her tenth margarita and can still remember her children's screams from the house fire.

ELSE

That is not Daddy.

That is someone **else** with his hand on Mommy's thigh.

EMPTY

Mother's purse is **empty**.

There is nothing in it.

Anna will have to try Nanny's instead if she wants to pay her dealer.

ENTHRALL

The big, strong workmen **enthrall** Daddy.

They captivate him.

He brings Deborah to watch them every day.

ERROR

The doctor made an **error**.

He used a fountain pen by mistake.

He meant to use a rectal thermometer.

EVIDENCE

Evidence is something that gets you into trouble.

Jim has burned the **evidence**.

EXPERIENCE

We learn from **experience**.

We learn from the things we go through.

Mr. Green's **experience** taught him not to sit in the front row of the porn theater.

FADE

The chalk marks are starting to **fade**.

The outline is starting to disappear.

Soon we will not be able to tell where they found Daddy.

FAIL, FAILURE

When we **fail**, we do not achieve the result we wanted.

Alan's suicide bombing mission was a **failure**.

Now he will have to sit here without any legs until the police arrive.

FAST, FASTER, FASTEST

Dick can run **fast**. He can run quickly.

Peter runs **faster**.

Tom runs the **fastest**.

Ernest is in a wheelchair and lags behind.

FAVORITE

Simon is Mother's **favorite**.

She likes him better than Julie.

Sure, Julie gets good grades and volunteers at the homeless shelter . . . but can she stand on her head?

EXERCISE

Which of your parents is your favorite? Make a list of reasons explaining your choice, and then show it to them both over breakfast. Perhaps your list will spark a fun family discussion.

FEAR, FEARFUL

Clementine has a **fear** of caves.

Caves frighten her.

She has been **fearful** of them ever since Daddy broke both of her legs and left her in one.

FEED

Maxine will **feed** Baby.

Maxine will give Baby some food.

She is saving him the gristle.

FENDER

The mud guard above the
wheel of a car is called
a **fender**.

When Fluffy got run
over, she became lodged between
the wheel and the **fender**.

FLAT

Baby is lying **flat**.

He is lying spread
out on his back,
exactly where he
landed.

FLEE

Kate must
flee town.

She must leave
town quickly.

Her pimp has
gone psycho.

FOREMOST

Which of Sonia's personalities will be **foremost** today?

Which of them will dominate?

We hope it will not be the nymphomaniac with poor hygiene.

FORGET

Did you **forget** to let the cat in?

Did you fail to remember to let the cat in before last night's blizzard?

FRUITION

Richard's idea came to **fruition**.

His hard work brought it into being.

Now he can see Mrs. Thompson sunbathe topless from every angle.

G

GAIN

Ann-Marie wants to **gain** weight.

She wants to increase her weight.

She has heard that Peter likes fatties.

GAME, GAMES

A **game** is a contest between two or more people.

There is always a winner of a **game**.

Here are some examples of different **games**:

checkers

tennis

child custody

sexual harassment suit

GET

Ray will **get** strawberries from the garden.

He will obtain the strawberries and bring them home.

Maybe Father will notice him then.

GLAD

Lucille is **glad** that Mommy died.

She is delighted.

The replacement Daddy bought for her is much more fun.

GO, GONE

Where did Ben **go**?

He was playing on the lawn but now he is not there.

He is **gone**.

GUESS

We may **guess** that Lionel lives beside the nuclear power plant.

We may deduce this from his unusually high number of testicles.

HEAR

Grandpa does not **hear** well.

He has a hard time understanding what people are saying.

Why do the people at the bank seem to think he is an old count?

HEAVY, HEAVIER, HEAVIEST

Bobby has a **heavy** bag.

The bag and its contents weigh many pounds.

Mother has a **heavier** bag.

It weighs more than Bobby's.

Dad has the **heaviest** bag.

It contains the torso.

HEAVY-DUTY

Emma will need some **heavy-duty** makeup.

She will need the extra-strong stuff to cover up this latest lesion.

HIDE, HIDING

Jayne found a place to **hide**.

She found a place to stay out of sight.

She is **hiding** until Daddy goes back to the bar.

HINDSIGHT

With **hindsight**, we might have done things differently.

Looking back, we might have installed a fire escape at the orphanage.

HONEST

Father has been **honest**.

He has told Hannah the truth.

It is the Tooth Fairy that has been touching her at night.

HORRIFIC

When we describe something as **horrific**, we mean it is ghastly.

The embalmers have made a **horrific** mistake.

HOUSE

A **house** is a building in which people live.

Here is our **house**.

Here is the maid's
house.

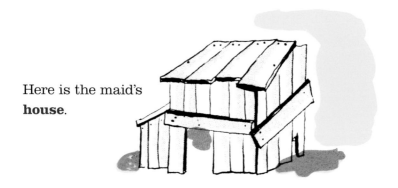

HURRAH

Oh **hurrah**!

Oh happy day!

Kate's new dildo is at least twice as big as her old one.

HYPOTHESIS

Annette has a **hypothesis**.

She has a theory that Baby will fly if she launches him from an upstairs window.

IDENTIFY

Ann helps Mother **identify** the perverts in the personal ads.

She helps Mother recognize the perverts, so that they can reply to them first.

IMPATIENT

Mr. Griffiths is getting **impatient**.

He cannot wait for his client to leave so that he can get back to banging his secretary.

IMPOSSIBLE

Mother's special birthday candles are **impossible** to blow out.

They cannot be blown out.

That should prevent Johnny's wishes for more slutty babysitters from coming true.

IMPRACTICAL

Donna's new locker is **impractical**.

It is not useful.

It has only one shelf, no lock, and no place to hang her inflatable boyfriend.

INCREASE

Jennie will **increase** her bet.

She will raise the value of her bet.

She will offer five dollars, her best dolly, and a blumpkin.

INSCRUTABLE

Topsy's blank stare is **inscrutable**.

We cannot know what she has witnessed.

Why did we have to get a rescue dog?

INTO

Abigail is putting the kitten **into** the basket.

She is placing the kitten inside the basket.

She is putting the basket **into** the river, just before the rapids.

JAM, JAMMED

Lucy is in a **jam**.

She is in a bind.

The dresser door is **jammed** shut.

This will be her last game of hide-and-go-seek.

JEALOUS

Ethel is **jealous**.

She feels envy as she reads the obituaries.

JOB

Lorna has a special **job**.

She has a special task to complete.

She is helping Mommy sneak the drugs through customs.

JOY

Joy is a feeling of great delight.

Ruby was filled with **joy** when she pushed Candice into the furnace.

KEEP

The medal is Jane's to **keep**.

It is Jane's to have, so long as she keeps her mouth shut about what she saw the principal doing in the parking lot last night.

KEEPSAKE

Paul's parents kept his tumor as a **keepsake**.

They kept it to remember him by.

KNIT

Mother will **knit** Alan a sweater.

She will make it using wool.

It will be just like he is still alive.

KNIFE, KNIVES

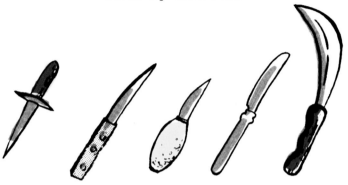

A **knife** is an instrument that has a blade.

Here is Mandy's secret collection of **knives**.

EXERCISE

*Help Mandy choose which **knife** to use for each task:*

1. Peeling potatoes.

2. Spreading butter.

3. Jimmying a lock on a car door.

4. Giving herself a cool-looking scar.

5. Finding out what is inside Fluffy.

KNOW

Gavin did not **know** that the label on the jar was wrong.

He was not aware that Mother had even kept her placenta.

LAST

Billy's horse finished **last**.

Billy's horse finished after all of the others.

LEFT

Very little of Alan was **left** after the explosion.

Very little of him remained.

LID

Tommy nails a **lid** onto the coffin.

The **lid** stops Snowball from getting out.

LIE, LIED, LYING

Jim told a **lie**.

He told an untruth.

He **lied** about his lifeguard training, and now Jess is **lying** dead at the bottom of the pool.

LIKE

Our snowman looks just **like** Mommy.

Its shape is the same as Mommy's, now that she has overcome her bulimia.

LIST

Sabrina made a **list** of reasons to live.

She catalogued the reasons.

There is nothing on her **list**.

EXERCISE

Make your own list of reasons to live. If, like Sabrina, you are unable to think of any, try writing a list of suicide methods instead.

LITERALLY

Walter took the meaning of the words **literally**.

He took the meaning of the words "doggy-style" at face value.

LIVE

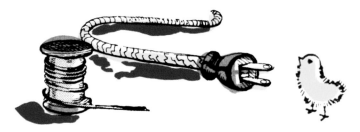

The wire is **live**.

It is full of electrical current.

Chico does not have long to **live**.

LIVEN

The factory tour has started to **liven** up.

It has become more interesting.

One of the workmen has been dragged into the machinery.

LOOSE, LOOSENED

Bobby's tooth is **loose**.

It can be moved.

Daddy **loosened** it with his fist.

LOOT, LOOTING

When we **loot**, we ransack and steal.

Granny's care workers are busy **looting** her upstairs rooms.

LUCK

Rodrigo cannot believe his **luck**.

He cannot believe his good fortune.

So many children to molest and not an adult in sight.

MAKE, MAKING, MADE

We put materials together when we **make** something.

Laura can **make** a dress.

Lizzie is **making** a cake.

By the end of the day, Jim will have **made** some glue.

MASK, MASKS

A **mask** is a false face.

Tommy and Kitty wear **masks** over their real faces when they torture their victims.

MATTER

What is the **matter** with Daddy?

What is wrong with Daddy?

Why is he not breathing? And why is he hanging from a belt in the closet?

MELLOW

Father's mood is **mellow**.

He is calm.

The beta blockers are finally kicking in.

METAPHOR

The wedding gift became a **metaphor**.

It became a symbol.

MISHEARD

Anne deliberately **misheard** what Father said.

She told herself that he is taking her skating.

He actually said that he is walking out on her and her two-bit whore of a mother.

MIX, MIXTURE

Hilary will **mix** pineapple and parsley.

She will blend them to make a drink.

The **mixture** is called an herbal abortion.

MODEL

A **model** is a representation of something.

Bert is making a **model** of a terrorist attack.

It will help him decide where to plant the real bomb.

MULTITASKING

Candice is **multitasking**.

She is highlighting Ruby's inadequacies while chipping away at her confidence, casting doubt on her parentage, and making a handy ashtray all at the same time.

NAME

Ella will **name** the doll Mommy.

She will call the doll Mommy.

Then she will ram a needle through it.

NERVOUS

Shirley is **nervous** about the talent show.

She is worried no one will like her striptease.

NEW

Rose has a **new** friend.

She met him today.

They are going to play for the first time.

NEWS

News tells us what is happening in the world.

Today's **news** is all about a local kidnapping.

Marjorie is glad to learn her new baby is on the way.

NIGHTMARE

Carol had a **nightmare**.

She had a bad dream that
Daddy had come
back to life
and was
trying to
shoot her again.

NINE

Heather has **nine** valentines.

One from each of the seven boys she slept with this week.

And the two girls.

NOISE, NOISY

Our band makes **noise**.

We make loud sounds.

When we are very **noisy**, we can hardly hear our parents screaming death threats at each other.

NONE

Francine is looking for some small sign that her life has meaning.

There is **none**.

There isn't one.

NOSTALGIC

Father is **nostalgic**.

He is remembering the happy times before you were born.

NOTED

The barber is **noted** in our town.

He is distinguished.

The police have put him on a register of sex offenders.

NOTORIOUS

Candice's character assassinations are **notorious**.

Whether focusing on a friend's personality flaws, dysfunctional family, or hereditary disease, they are famously vicious.

NOW

The lamp was on the table.

Now it is on the floor.

Bowser was a naughty dog.

Now he is no more.

NUISANCE

The neighbors' dog is a **nuisance**.

He is a pest.

We have put a poisoned sausage in the garden.

OBLIVION

Oblivion is an empty void.

It can be found by drinking lots of vodka.

In **oblivion**, it does not matter so much if you walked out on your terminally ill husband.

OLD

We have a new mommy and daddy.

Our **old** mommy and daddy tried to drown us in the creek.

ONCE

Keith will have the urn valued **once** he has cleaned it.

He will have it valued as soon as he has rinsed out the last of Mother's ashes.

ONLY

Only Moira can hear Baby's thoughts.

No one but Moira can hear where Baby wants to be buried.

OPPORTUNE

The flood came at an **opportune** time.

It came at an appropriate moment.

Sheila and Antony had already knocked Grandma unconscious and locked her in the cellar.

ORDER

Father asked Mary to carry out some chores in **order**.

First, she must pour a bottle of bleach down her little brother's throat.

Second, she must jump off of the roof.

ORDINARY

Wendy feels **ordinary**.

She feels less special since she found out about Michael's other wife.

OUT

Mother says she is going **out**.

She says she is leaving the house to buy some groceries.

OVERCOMPENSATING

Steve is **overcompensating**.

His fear of aging has driven him into the arms of younger and younger women.

OVERNIGHT

Uncle Dean works **overnight**.

He goes to work during the night.

PACT

James and Harriet have made a **pact**.

They have made an agreement.

If Father does not stop beating them, they will slash their wrists all over his new car seats.

PARANOID

Lorna is **paranoid**.

She is overly suspicious.

Rex is not even trained to sniff out drugs.

PARK

A **park** is a garden that is open to the public.

cruising ground

pedophile

victim

stolen baby

drunk

abandoned
pet

PICKY

Scruffy is not **picky**.

He will give anybody's leg a go.

PLAN

Joseph has a **plan**.

He has worked out a scheme to become an only child.

PLAUSIBLE

Harold makes a **plausible** dentist.

He is quite convincing at first.

POCKETBOOK

Anna dips into Mother's **pocketbook**.

It is a small bag used for carrying money and Xanax.

PORCH

A **porch** is a sheltered area at the front of a house.

Mother has passed out on the **porch** after too many mint juleps.

PRAY, PRAYING

When we **pray**, we ask God for help.

Gertrude is **praying** that Father Logan will get raped in jail.

She wants him to know how it feels.

PREFER

Which does Clara **prefer**?

Which does she like more?

Cookies or crystal meth?

PREPARE

Mother is helping Stephanie **prepare** for her date tonight.

She is helping Stephanie get ready.

She is making sure the clasp on Stephanie's bra is nice and loose for easy access.

PRESENTABLE

We will make Ruffles **presentable** again.

We will wash all the blood out of his fur and hope that no one notices he isn't breathing.

PRETTY

The flames are **pretty**.

They make the school look nice.

And they make all the hurt go away.

PRICE

Everything has a **price**.

It has a monetary value.

Samantha's **price** is $100, with discounts on slow nights.

PRIEST

A **priest** is a kind of child molester who hides out in a church.

Where do you think the **priest** is hiding?

PROGRESS, PROGRESSED

If something makes **progress**, it moves forward.

Tommy started with small animals before he **progressed** to human victims.

PROPITIOUS

What a **propitious** start to the day!

What a promising start!

The sun is shining and Gramps has settled for a hand job.

PROUD

Peter is **proud** of his work.

He is pleased with his work.

He feels certain no one will find Carol Ann this time.

EXERCISE

Write a story about Peter using all of these P words: plant, petal, pebble, path, patella, putrefied, police, prison.

PUMP

A **pump** is a device for controlling the flow of water or air.

Jane's stomach **pump** produced a pint of tequila, several of her own teeth, and a used condom.

PUPPY, PUPPIES

A **puppy** is a young dog.

Connie gets a puppy every time she agrees not to tell.

Daddy calls them hush **puppies**.

PUT

Put down the knife, Grandma.

Lay down the knife.

QUARREL, QUARRELLING

When you **quarrel**, you argue with someone.

Stuart and Helena are **quarrelling** about who left Baby unsupervised in the yard.

QUICK, QUICKLY

Quick! Make haste!

We must get to the hospital **quickly** if we want to be included in Grandma's will.

RATHER

Mother would **rather** you were quiet.

She would prefer that you keep your muzzle on for now.

RAVENOUS

Fido is **ravenous**.

He is so hungry he could eat anything.

REACH

The antidote is out of Jerry's **reach**.

He cannot touch it because it is too high.

REASONABLE

Another round of golf seems **reasonable** to Ted.

It seems sensible.

After all, it is not the first time the doctors have described Martha as "slipping away."

REDUNDANT

The toys are **redundant**.

They are no longer necessary.

Paul has not played with them since he lost his motor functions.

REGRET

Jemima is starting to **regret** letting Joseph row her out to the middle of the lake.

She wishes she had not allowed it.

She does not like the look in Joseph's eyes.

RELENTLESS

Mandy is **relentless**.

Once she starts killing, she cannot stop.

REMEMBER

When we **remember**, we think back.

Bert is trying to **remember** how to tie a noose.

REMOVE, REMOVED

The repo men **remove** Kathy's belongings.

The repo men take her belongings away.

Kathy has **removed** her underwear in an attempt to keep her favorite chair.

REQUIRE, REQUIRES

What does Andrew **require** to make a party favor for Anna?

What does Andrew need?

He **requires** a cardboard tube, some shiny paper, and a dead rat.

RESORT

Maggie is Daddy's last **resort**.

He only wants to molest her when all the other children are busy.

RETICULOENDOTHELIOSIS

Nobody noticed the Little Red Hen had **reticuloendotheliosis**.

Nobody noticed her diarrhea and leg weakness.

REVOLVER

A **revolver** is a gun that is small enough to fit in your schoolbag.

S

SACRIFICE

To **sacrifice** something is to give it up.

We begin our rituals with a human **sacrifice**.

SAD

Louise is **sad**.

She is mournful.

If Spot has really gone to live on a farm, why is his tail sticking up out of the ground?

SAFE

I felt **safe** when I went with the policeman.

I felt out of danger.

Until he handcuffed me to a pipe in this abandoned warehouse.

SCARE

Paul had a **scare** on Halloween

He had a fright.

The doctors told him he had leukemia.

SCRAPBOOK

Mary pastes pictures into her **scrapbook**.

It is a book of photographs and memories that make her impossibly tedious life seem worthwhile.

**pregnant by
local butcher**

Oedipal

**killed local
butcher and minced
the body**

SECRET, SECRETS

A **secret** is something you do not want people to know about.

Every family is full of **secrets**.

prefers girls

prefers
animals

SENSITIVE

Sometimes Father is not very **sensitive**.

Sometimes he is not aware of people's feelings.

Of all the days to start abusing Susie, he should have thought twice about it on her birthday.

SET, SETTINGS

Grace will **set** the table.

She will put out five **settings**.

Surely Daddy cannot stay away forever.

SHORT

Matthew is **short** one block.

He is in need of one block.

SIGNATURE

Molly requires Rhona's **signature**.

She requires Rhona to sign her name to indicate that Molly cannot be held responsible if the abortion goes wrong.

SILENCE

Dwight tries to **silence** Jeanette.

He tries to stop her from talking.

She clearly does not recognize his wife.

SIMILAR

If things are **similar**, they are alike.

These two cars are **similar**.

Lawn and **loan** are similar words.

They sound **similar**.

EXERCISE

Choose from the two similar-sounding words to complete the sentences:

1. The clown will **amuse / abuse** the children.

2. Lana used a marker pen to **deface / debase** herself.

3. Mother will not tolerate **insects / incest** in her kitchen.

4. John has written an essay about his **heroes / herpes**.

5. Daddy keeps his **horse / whores** in a stable behind the house.

SKYSCRAPER

This is a **skyscraper**.

It is a building tall enough to throw yourself from to punish your loved ones for not caring enough.

SMALL, SMALLEST

Susie is **small**.

She is not big enough to reach the table.

As the **smallest** member of the family, she has to snort her coke off of a chair.

SMUGGLE

We will **smuggle** in something sharp for Daddy.

We will sneak it past the prison guards.

SOUND, SOUNDS

Gillian hears a **sound** in the basement.

It **sounds** like someone crying.

Where has Momma gone?

SOUNDLY

Hilary sleeps **soundly**.

She sleeps peacefully
since the abortion.

SPOT

Can you **spot** the rapist?

Can you see him?

He is hiding behind the tree,
waiting for an old lady to come along.

STICKY

The stain is **sticky**.

It is tacky like glue.

Alice is never using the bathtub after Jack again.

STILL

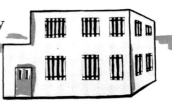

Giles is standing **still** while we turn him into a snowman.

At first, he would not stop shivering.

Now he is nice and motionless.

STRICT

Mandy's new school is very **strict**.

Its rules are very firm.

She will not be allowed out on another killing spree.

STROKE

Kitty is having a **stroke**. Her fur is being petted.

Grandpa is having a **stroke**. His brain is degenerating.

STUBBORN

Father's bloodstains are **stubborn**.

They will not come out no matter how hard Mother scrubs.

SUDDENLY

Paul is **suddenly** very popular.

He has become popular rapidly.

Now that he is in a coma, his parents are giving away all his toys to his closest friends.

SULK

Do not **sulk**, Simon.

Do not mope.

You can tell us all about your brittle bone disease when we finish skating.

SURPRISE

Philip has a **surprise** for his wife.

He has an unexpected treat.

He has bought a new dress.

In his size.

SUSPECT

Does Ted **suspect** anything is going on between his wife and Roger?

Does the son of a bitch know more than he is letting on?

T

TAKE

If we **take** something, we make it ours.

TALENT

A **talent** is a special ability.

Dorothy has a **talent**.

She can tell who was sitting in a chair by sniffing it.

TARDY

Connie is **tardy**.

She is late.

She wishes Daddy would wait until after school to abuse her.

TEST

Myrtle will **test** Alice's claim.

She will find out if Alice's peanut allergy really *is* fatal.

THROW, THROWING, THREW, THROWN

See Uncle Bob **throw** Mandy.

He sends her through the air.

He is **throwing** her now.

He **threw** her high.

He has **thrown** her into the river.

THROAT

The **throat** is the front part of the neck.

Jane has a very pretty **throat**.

It is just slender enough to get both hands around.

TIE, TIED

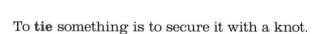

To **tie** something is to secure it with a knot.

Mother does not want to be **tied** down by a family.

She would rather be **tied** up by a stranger.

TIGHT, TIGHTER, TIGHTEST

The buckle keeps the belt **tight**. It keeps it fixed in place.

You can wear the belt **tighter** if you have a smaller waist.

You can wear it at its **tightest** during autoerotic asphyxiation.

TIME, TIMING

Chico has picked a bad **time** to hatch.

His **timing** is poor.

TOGETHER

Frank, Joan, and Betty bathe **together**.

They bathe at the same time.

Thanks to the ecstasy, they have lots of fun **together**.

TOY

A **toy** is something to play with.

Matthew thought that the gun was a **toy**.

The hole in his sister's forehead suggests otherwise.

TRIUMPH

Milly's plan was a **triumph**.

It was a success.

One roller skate on
the stairs and
now there will
be no new baby.

UNDER

The cocaine bugs have gotten **under** Patty's skin.

They have gotten beneath the surface.

She cannot seem to wash them out.

UNTIE

An **untie** is a cross between an uncle and an auntie.

My **untie** is making me some tea.

UNTIL

Ricky played in the attic **until** nine o'clock.

He played up to that time.

Then he began to wonder when Mother would be back with the key.

UNTRACEABLE

Shellfish toxin is **untraceable**.

It cannot be found by the coroner.

UPSIDE

Most situations have an **upside**.

They have a benefit.

The **upside** of Alan's death is that his brother can have the top bunk.

VALUE

Mother's wedding ring has a high **value**.

It is worth a lot of money.

It will fund her divorce lawyer.

VARIATION

Jack uses his left hand for **variation**.

It keeps things interesting on the lonely nights.

VARIETY

The photographs show Mother in a **variety** of poses.

They show her in all kinds of positions.

VIE

The children **vie** for Mother's affections.

They compete for her affections.

She only has enough love for three.

VISIT

Mother will go **visit** her best friend.

She will go see the man whose little bottles of pills make the day bearable.

VOICE, VOICES

Every night, Tommy hears a **voice**.

He hears someone talking inside his head.

The **voices** tell him who must die next.

WAIT

Daddy's secret friend will **wait** in the car.

She will stay in the car until Mother has left for work.

WARNING

Lynn gave Natalie a **warning**.

She cautioned Natalie: "Stay away from Roland or I will give you crabs."

WAVE

Chip likes to **wave** at the cars as they go by.

He likes to move his hand up and down.

Sometimes the drivers **wave** back.

WEAPON, WEAPONS

A **weapon** causes injury or death.

baseball bat

boiling water

scissors

hammer

crank

WEARY

Scruffy is **weary**.

He is tired from playing with Carol Ann.

It took a lot of effort to dig her up.

WHEN

Karen will take the last pill **when** she hears the ambulance.

She will take the last pill at that time.

WISH, WISHED, WISHES

Brian made a **wish**.

He **wished** he was in Carla's pants.

Carla made a **wish**.

She **wishes** the itching would stop.

WITHOUT

Annette came back from her stroll **without** Baby.

Baby was not with Annette anymore.

She gave Baby to a nice man at the park.

WOMAN

Mother is a **woman**.

Grandma is a **woman**.

Mike wants to be a **woman**.

WONDER

Trudy is starting to **wonder**.

She is starting to question what was in the root beer float that Uncle Rory made for her.

WRONG, WRONGLY

Isabel was **wrong**.

She was mistaken.

She **wrongly** thought that she was going to work for her father's brother.

In fact, she is going to work for her father's *brothel*.

new crack pipe

bong

month's food

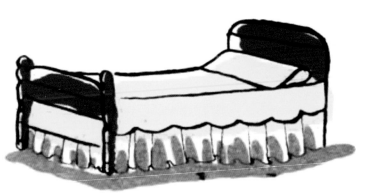

**two months' rent on
scummy apartment**

cheap whore

porn DVD

quarter of weed

WORTH

Ian is calculating how much his furniture is **worth**.

He is calculating how much money he will get for his furniture when he sells it to fund his new lifestyle.

8-ball of cocaine

very cheap whore

X-RAY

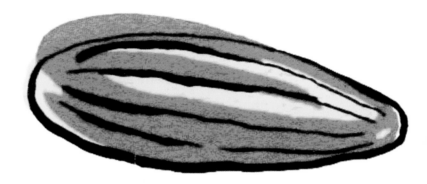

An **x-ray** machine lets doctors see inside your body.

Marjorie had an **x-ray** of her pelvis to find out where the cucumber was lodged.

Y

YAWN, YAWNING

We **yawn** when we are tired.

We open our mouths wide to get more oxygen.

When Alex started **yawning**, Uncle Bob knew that the Rohypnol was starting to kick in.

YES

When we say "**yes**" to something, it means we agree to it.

Mother said "**yes**" before she found out that Father was a wife-beater.

ZEAL, ZEALOUSLY

Mark performed his task with **zeal**.

He performed it with enthusiasm.

He **zealously** hacked Robin up after the argument.

ZERO

Zero means nothing.

The doctors have given Paul a **zero** chance of survival.

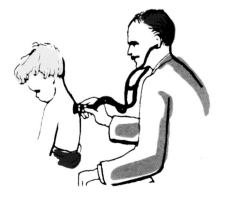

ZIGZAG

A **zigzag** is a jagged line.

We can tell that Mother has been drinking when she drives in a **zigzag** pattern.

ZOO

A **zoo** is a place where people can go
to look at animals.

Daddy takes us to the **zoo** every weekend now that he has joint custody.

THANK, THANKFUL, THANKS

To **thank** people is to express how grateful you are to them. Ross would like to **thank** his agent, Matt McGowan, without whom this book would never have happened, and Kate Hamill, whose keen editing made it the best it could be.

Ross is also **thankful** to John LaSala and the Very Us Artists, as well as Shayne Zucker and Tim Harrod.

His love and **thanks** go to Matthew Browne, Eileen Horsley, David Horsley, and Lorna Horsley.

ABOUT THE AUTHOR

Ross Horsley is a mild-mannered librarian at the Leeds Local and Family History Library in England by day . . . and a watcher of gruesome slasher movies by night. Visit his website, MyFirstDictionary.blogspot.com.

FLASH CARDS

Cut out and keep these handy flash cards to test your vocabulary, recall, and spelling. Perhaps you could rearrange them and use them to write a story of your own.